W9-CGX-326

From Pond to Prairie

LAURENCE PRINGLE

From

Pond to Prairie

The Changing World of a Pond and Its Life

Illustrated by Karl W. Stuecklen

THE MACMILLAN COMPANY
New York, New York
Collier-Macmillan Limited, London

For Sean, who likes to help
his father drive

The author wishes to thank David F. Costello, the author of *Prairie World,* for reading and suggesting changes in the manuscript of this book.

 Library of Congress catalog card number: 70–175599. The Macmillan Company, 866 Third Avenue, New York, N.Y. 10022. Collier-Macmillan Canada Ltd., Toronto, Ontario. Printed in the United States of America. 1 2 3 4 5 6 7 8 9 10

Contents

A Pond on the Prairie

It is a hot summer day on the prairie. A red-tailed hawk spins slowly in the sky, searching the land below for food.

The hawk soars over level plains, gently rolling hills, tree-lined streams—all part of the vast prairies that once covered much of the Central United States and adjoining parts of Canada. One third of North America originally was prairie.

This land was once a sea of grass where bison, wolves, and pronghorn antelopes thrived. Man has changed that. There is little wild prairie left. Today, a soaring hawk looks down on cattle, not bison, and on vast fields of wheat, not wild grasses.

To a hawk, though, these changes may not seem so great. There are still ground squirrels and prairie voles to catch. There are still some prairie-dog towns. And here and there, tucked in the folds of the rolling hills, are prairie ponds.

Some ponds cover many acres and hold enough water to support a fringe of willow trees around their edges. Others are small and may be full of water for only a few months, after the spring rains. Some ponds have been recently dug by man, using a bulldozer. Others were dug thousands of years ago, by a great sheet of ice called a *glacier*.

But all of the ponds are alike in some ways. They are a source of water in a dry land—almost like an oasis in a desert. Because of this they are a magnet for wild animals of many kinds. And life goes on in these ponds much as it did centuries ago, before man tamed the prairies.

Some prairie ponds have disappeared—drained of their waters so that man could plant crops on the land. Thousands of other ponds are also vanishing, but in a much slower, much more fascinating way.

These ponds vanish by changing into something else—as every pond and lake on earth does eventually. The changes are not quick. They take place over hundreds or thousands of years.

This book tells how a pond slowly changes until it becomes a prairie. Beyond the prairies, forests usually grow where ponds used to be. But ponds everywhere go through most of the same stages as they slowly vanish. No matter where you live, you can find a pond that is changing much as a prairie pond does.

New Pond-
New Life

Whether it is dug by man or by a glacier, a newly formed pond has little life in it. The bottom may be sand, poor soil, or even bare rock. The pond slowly fills with water from rain or melting ice and snow.

Before long, some living things appear in the water. Many of them are too small to be seen without a microscope. We can only guess at where many of them come from. Some one-celled animals may be carried into the pond when rain water trickles off the land into the pond. Others, such as the simple plants called *bacteria*, may drop into the pond from the air.

The tiny drifting plants and animals are called *plankton*. Some plankton are plants called *algae*. With energy from the sun, the algae make their own food. Some of this energy is passed along when plankton animals eat algae.

Once plankton are plentiful in the pond, many other kinds of living things can survive there. The food energy from plankton is passed along to water insects, small shrimp, and young fish. Larger animals feed on the insects, shrimp, and small fish. Food energy is passed from one organism to another. Each living thing, from a tiny plant to a big fish or a raccoon, is like a link in a chain—a chain of food energy.

As time goes on, more and more living things find a home in the pond. Insects, such as dragonflies, fly in from nearby bodies of water. Other life may be brought to the

pond by birds such as herons and ducks. Mud on their feet may contain plant seeds and the eggs of insects or even fish. When the birds hunt for food at the new pond, they accidentally bring new life with them.

In just a few years, the new pond becomes a lively place, rich with animal life. Some kinds of animals spend most of their lives on or near the bottom. Watch in the shallow water along the shore. You may see bluegill sunfish guarding nests on the clear bottom. You may also see insects crawling along the bottom or swimming through the water. Fresh-water clams (mussels) also move slowly

along the bottom, straining plankton from the water. At one time or another in their lives, the survival of all of these animals depends on the bare bottom of the pond.

As the years pass, a layer of dark, mucky soil begins to build up on the bottom. Some soil may be washed into the water from the surrounding land, but most of it is made up of partly decayed plants and animals. Each year millions of the short-lived plankton die and settle to the bottom of the pond. Leaves from plants along the pond's edge drop into the water and begin to decay. The body of an insect, a dead fish, a bird's feather—all drift down to the bottom and gradually become part of a layer of mucky soil there.

Slowly the soil builds up on the pond bottom. It may take a hundred years for a half-inch to form.

Eventually the kinds of animals whose lives depend on the clear bottom die out. They are replaced by other kinds of animals that can live on a bottom covered with soil and decaying material.

The steady build-up of soil and dead material on the bottom provides nourishment and living places for different kinds of plants and animals. For the first time, plants with roots can grow underwater in great numbers. Changing from its "young" stage, the pond next develops an underwater jungle of submerged plants. Other plants begin to creep out from the shore. The pond is slowly beginning to vanish.

A Jungle Underwater

In the deepest parts of the pond, little sunlight may reach the pond floor. Closer to shore, however, sunlight filters through a forest of green plants rooted in the bottom soil. The plants include pond weed, hornwort, water crowfoot, and water milfoil (whose name means "thousand leaves").

From a canoe or rowboat, you can reach overboard and pull up a handful of these long, stringy plants. They hang limp in your hand and break easily. These plants spend all their lives underwater (although some kinds have flowers that grow just above the surface). The water is their support. They don't need the tough structure of trees and other plants that live in the air.

Look on the stems and leaves of these plants for animal life. You may find snails clinging there. They eat leaves, or algae that grow on the plants. The snails lay clusters of eggs on the plant stems. In two or three weeks, dozens or even hundreds of tiny snails hatch. Many of them become food for other animals. Only a few live long enough to grow into adults and to lay eggs of their own.

Although most underwater plants provide food and shelter for animals, one kind of plant traps and kills them. The *bladderwort* has many small baglike traps. Each trap has a slitlike opening, edged with bristling hairs. Some of these hairs act as guides, leading insects or other small animals closer to the entrance of the trap. Other hairs act as triggers.

The trap is set when the entrance is closed and the sides of the bag are pushed in. When an insect or other small animal touches a trigger hair, the trap opens. Water rushes in, carrying the animal along with it. Chemicals inside slowly digest the food. As this happens, some water passes out through the walls of the trap. This sets the trap for another victim.

Above the bladderworts float the leaves of water lilies. They may cover the entire surface of a shallow pond. Water lilies usually don't grow in water that is deeper than six feet. Water-lily stems are as flexible as rope, allowing the leaves to float freely, rising and falling as the water level changes.

The broad, waxy leaves provide homes and hiding places for many animals. Turn a leaf over and look at its

underside. You may find a snail, tiny water mites, the eggs of water insects, or a caterpillar that feeds only on the leaves of water lilies.

Frogs sit on the broad leaves by day. You can hear their calls if you visit the pond on a spring or summer night. The deep croaks of a bullfrog sound like "jug-o-rum," while the green frog's call is like the twang of a banjo.

Day or night, the pond seems to be a peaceful place. But beneath the quiet surface there are ambushes, chases, and killings. A giant water bug grasps a small fish in its strong forelegs, then sucks out its juices. A snapping turtle lunges up and grabs a young duck. In the shadows of the water-lily leaves, a sharp-toothed pickerel waits for a smaller fish to swim by.

The pond is like a community, with a job for each living thing. Some are *plant-eaters*, some are *meat-eaters*, and some (such as bacteria and fungi) are *decomposers*—breaking down the remains of dead plants and animals. When this happens, some minerals and other substances are freed. They may be taken into a plant's roots or leaves. Then the cycle starts all over again, where it began, with the *food-producers*—the green plants.

Each year the cycle of life in the pond slows down as winter comes. The stems and leaves of most water plants die, but the roots, buds, and seeds live on, ready to produce new life in the spring. The stems and leaves settle to the bottom and begin to decay, adding to the mucky ooze there. Little by little, the soil on the pond bottom grows deeper and the water gets shallower.

The Edge Creeps In

Close to shore, in only a foot or so of water, are plants that are quite different from those that grow completely underwater. These plants are rooted in the mucky soil but have tough stems and their leaves are held above the water. Because of this, they are called *emergents*. They include spike rushes, arrowheads, and pickerelweeds.

A short distance away grow other kinds of emergent plants—cattails, reeds, and bulrushes. You can find them along the shore edge, either on land or in the shallow water.

The emergent plants form a ring around the pond. Life in this zone is different from that in the deeper waters. Soil and decaying material build up fastest along the pond edge. As the dead plants decay, bacteria take a great deal of oxygen from the water.

There may be so little oxygen that some kinds of fish and other animals can't survive. The snails that live among the emergent plants are usually lung-breathers. They renew their air supply by climbing to the surface on a plant stem.

The stalks and stems of emergent plants are important to the lives of many animals. Diving spiders rest there, then plunge into the water after insects. Female dragonflies and damselflies land on stalks near the surface, put the rear of their bodies underwater, and lay eggs on the stalks. The eggs will hatch only underwater.

You may find a young dragonfly, or *nymph,* clinging to a plant stem underwater. These fierce-looking, wingless insects are deadly hunters, catching many kinds of water insects and even small fish. When some live food comes near a nymph, the insect flicks its big jaw forward. A pair of sharp hooks at the tip of the jaw stab the prey. Then the nymph's jaw folds back, carrying the food to its mouth.

After a year or more underwater, the nymph climbs up a plant stem into the air. The back of its nymph skin splits open, and an adult dragonfly wiggles out. After its wings stretch and dry, the adult flies off, hunting mosquitoes and other small insects.

You may see the dry, empty nymph skins of dragonflies and damselflies on plant stalks if you walk along the pond edge in summer. (You usually have to get up very early to actually see the insect breaking free of its old skin.) On the surface of the water you may see other insects, including water striders, which run on "tiptoe" over the water,

and whirligig beetles, which have special eyes that enable them to see above and below water at the same time.

There's always a lot to see along the pond edge. Raccoons know that there is good hunting there. Look in the mud for the handlike tracks of these mammals. You may find a partly eaten frog or crayfish—a sign that a raccoon's hunt was successful.

Look also for the tracks of long-legged wading birds such as herons. By day they hunt the same shallows where raccoons busily search at night. Herons stalk slowly through the water, or stand and wait for food to swim to them. Then there is a quick stab with a sharp beak, a

swallow, and the heron stands motionless again.

Each year, bit by bit, parts of plants and animals settle to the bottom and are slowly changed into soil that takes the place of water. The pond gets shallower. The emergent plants creep in toward the center of the pond. The pond gets smaller. Cattails grow where the water was once deep enough for water lilies. And there is solid land, covered with prairie grasses, where cattails once grew.

All this happens slowly. It may take hundreds or thousands of years. But one day the pond is gone. The water that remains is so shallow that only emergent plants grow in it. The pond has changed into something else—a marsh.

The Magic of a Marsh

A marsh in early morning is alive with sound. The calls of frogs blend with those of ducks and blackbirds. But one sound catches and holds your attention. It is like a monstrous machine slowly starting up, right there in the wild marsh.

The loud pumping sound is made by an American bittern, a brown and white wading bird about the size of a chicken. Even though you hear the bittern's call, you may never see the bird. A bittern usually stands very still. The brown and white stripes on its body match the background of cattail leaves.

Cattails, sedges, and rushes bend and sway in the prairie breezes. Now there are only small areas of open water among the emergent plants. If you step into the water, your foot touches what looks like the bottom—and keeps going down through the mucky ooze. The real bottom of firm soil may be a foot or two below the top of the decaying material.

In a handful of this muck you'll find worms, insects, and many other small animals. Too small to be seen, bacteria and fungi are breaking down the dead leaves and other material. With so much decay going on there is little oxygen in the water. Catfish are the only fish that survive. They can live with little oxygen. They find food in the bottom muck with the sensitive whiskerlike barbels around their mouths.

Above the quiet water, red-winged blackbirds perch on cattail leaves and sway with them. Each male red-wing calls out *konk-ka-ree*, warning other males that his nest and mate are nearby. Marsh wrens also build their nests among the cattails and reeds. There is plenty of insect food for birds in the marsh.

You may find some cattail leaves lying in the water, or a whole plant floating free, its roots showing. This is the work of muskrats. These rodents eat cattails and live in lodges made from the leaves of cattails and other marsh plants.

Inside the snug lodges, muskrats are usually safe from their enemies. Even mink, which eat many muskrats, seldom attack healthy muskrats in their dens. Mink usually kill the muskrats that are easiest to catch—old, sick, or injured ones.

Muskrats produce many young each year. If most of

the young survive, the muskrat population grows quickly. Sometimes muskrats get so plentiful that food becomes scarce. They fight among themselves, sometimes killing each other. Many die of disease. Once the population decreases enough, life returns to normal.

Outside its lodge, a muskrat may become food for a red-tailed hawk that plunges down from high in the sky, or for a marsh hawk that swoops low overhead. The marsh hawk hovers and glides just above the cattails and surprises many mice, muskrats, and other rodents. Its nest is on the ground in the marsh or among the tall prairie grasses nearby.

Ducks also nest in the marsh. In summer, female pintails, mallards, gadwalls, and teal glide along the surface,

each trailed by a row of ducklings. In spring and fall, ducks by the hundreds spill out of the sky and settle on the marsh. They rest and feed there before continuing their long migration.

Watch one of these ducks for a few minutes. Suddenly it seems to capsize. Its tail goes up and its head disappears underwater. Then it turns upright again. This is called *dabbling,* but it is not play. The duck eats seeds, insects, and leaves while its head is underwater.

Dabbling ducks can only reach about a foot and a half below the surface. So the shallow waters of the prairie marsh are just right for them and are a home from spring thaw to autumn ice.

In years of little rain, the marsh may dry up. When the rains come again, they are too late to save the lives of catfish, tadpoles, and many water insects. But others survive. Snails and crayfish bury themselves in the mud. The eggs of tiny shrimp and plankton have tough coats that keep them from drying out. When the rains come, the marsh springs to life again.

Each year the marsh gets a little smaller, a little shallower. It gradually disappears as the pond did before. The last cattail dies and its place is taken by a sunflower, or a clump of Indian grass. The animals and plants whose lives depended on the watery marsh world are gone. The life of the prairie takes over.

Where a Pond Used to Be

Little rain falls on the prairie, and the winter wind can be bitterly cold. The animals that live there are especially suited for life in this open sea of grass.

There are few hiding places above ground, so many prairie animals live in burrows. Badgers, prairie dogs, ground squirrels, and gophers dig dens deep in the soil. These shelters are often used by snakes and burrowing owls.

Some prairie animals rely on speed, instead of burrows, to escape their enemies. Pronghorn antelope can run about 50 miles per hour for a few minutes, covering the ground in 20-foot leaps. Jack rabbits are almost as fast. Coyotes sometimes work in teams to catch a jack rabbit, with one chasing the rabbit while another waits in ambush.

The lives of all prairie animals depend on the prairie plants, including shrubs, herbs, and grasses. Needle grass, little bluestem, blue grama, plains muhly, panic grass, buffalo grass—these are just a few of the many kinds of grass that grow on the prairies of North America.

Some of these grow where the pond used to be. Their roots reach down and take minerals from soil that formed on the pond bottom, hundreds of years ago. The minerals become part of the grass leaves. Later, a beetle eats some grass and the minerals become part of its body.

A bobolink seizes the beetle and swallows it. Then the bird rises in the air and sings its bubbly song, high over a place on the prairie where bison once drank, where herons hunted, where muskrats swam—the place where a pond used to be.

Index